Tony and Tessa were in their garden.
They were looking at the birds.

There were sparrows, a blackbird and some other birds.
They were all on the grass.

Tessa put the names of all the birds in a book.
She wanted to keep a book about all the birds
that came into the garden.

A cat came into the garden.
It wanted the birds.

Tony and Tessa saw the cat.
It jumped out!
All the birds flew away.

'The birds will not come into the garden now,' said Tessa.
She was not happy.
She wanted to look at the birds.

Tony put his coat on and went out.

When he came home he said, 'I want you to help me, Tessa.'
They went into the garden.
There was a box on the grass.

'What do you want me to do?' asked Tessa.
Tony opened the box.

'A bird table!' said Tessa.
'The birds will come into the garden now!'
Tony and Tessa began to put up the bird table.

Their mother looked out.
'Do you want some help?'
shouted their mother.

'Yes,' they said.
Their mother came out to help.

They were tired when the bird table was finished, but they were happy.
They put some food on the bird table.

They went inside and looked out of the window.
'Look!' shouted Tessa. 'Look at all the birds!'

The birds flew up to the table and had the food.
Tony and Tessa looked at the birds.
Tessa put the names of the birds in her book.

The cat came into the garden.
It looked up at the birds on the bird table.
The cat went away!